HAPPY BIRTHDAY, NICANOR PARRA

Other Books by Jim Smith

Surface Structures (St. Lawrence College/Kingston Writers Association, 1979)

Virus (Underwhich Editions, 1983)

One Hundred Most Frightening Things (blewointmentpress, 1985)

Convincing Americans (Proper Tales Press, 1986)

Crinoid Hill (The Front Press, 1986)

The Schwarzenegger Poems (Surrealist Poets' Gardening Assoc., 1988)

Telegrams (Proper Tales Press Blind Date, 1988)

INCLU OUR COMPE (Front Press, 1989)

Translating Sleep (Wolsak and Wynn, 1989)

Head Cutter (The Front Press Manuscript Editions, 1992)

Seven Pieces of Dream for Nora Astorga (The Front Press Manuscript Editions, 1992)

Daddee (The Front Press Manuscript Editions, 1993)

Sandino for Kids (The Front Press Manuscript Editions, 1993)

Leonel/Roque (Coteau Books, 1998)

Back Off, Assassin! New and Selected Poems (Mansfield Press, 2009)

Exit Interviews (Apt. 9 Press, 2011)

HAPPY BIRTHDAY, NICANOR PARRA

JIM SMITH

26·12·12

for Peter

with a big hug!

for a terrific guy!

¡Venceremos.

Jim Smith

MANSFIELD PRESS

Library and Archives Canada Cataloguing in Publication

Smith, Jim, 1951-
    Happy birthday, Nicanor Para / Jim Smith.

Poems.
Issued also in electronic formats.
ISBN 978-1-894469-86-9

    I. Title.

PS8637.M564H36 2012   C811'.54   C2012-906017-8

Editor for the Press: Stuart Ross
Design: Denis De Klerck
Typesetting: Stuart Ross
Cover Art: *El Asalto de la Máquina a las Fuerzas de la Destrucción*, by Eugenio Tellez
Author Photo: Jo-Anne McNamara

The publication of *Happy Birthday, Nicanor Parra* has been generously supported by
the Canada Council for the Arts and the Ontario Arts Council.

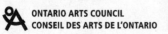

ONTARIO ARTS COUNCIL
CONSEIL DES ARTS DE L'ONTARIO

Canada Council   Conseil des Arts
for the Arts   du Canada

Mansfield Press Inc.
25 Mansfield Avenue, Toronto, Ontario, Canada M6J 2A9
Publisher: Denis De Klerck
www.mansfieldpress.net

Contents

for Mister Blue

Jim Smith's *Refugee Math*: The First Review

Smith clambers aboard the well-worn hobby-horse parked outside his
last publisher, & paper sword in hand, Pound's *Cantos* on the seat to
make him taller, thrashes away much like his description of his dog
in the mosh pit in last year's *Stuff I Did the Year Before*.

If you've seen one Smith whipping boy, you'll marvel that little has
changed and despite how many fascists fall to some sketchy *deus
ex machina*, three more pop up for every one burst like a bug on a
cottage zapper.

What redeems this latest quaint assemblage is that Smith was the
first to predict last week's Nazi colony on the moon. Few would have
called that one!

The Space Opera

Nicanor appears in the southern sky, growing every second.
A coup happens. A coup unhappens.
Deep beneath the Atacama Desert, lair of the rebels.
North America occupies 90% of the sky above Santiago.
The indigenous people are aliens.
The only way out of La Moneda is suicide.
Every night, a gun rises in the east, sets in the west.
A small fishing boat rescues flop-eared Jesus, drunk to the gills.
Jesus is a mercenary with a dark, dark past.
Nicanor points to the eventual heat death of the universe.

Gumby in uniform, clay gun at the ready.
Pinochet flees into old age.
Chile smells itself.
Nicanor sings softly in the nearest café.

No Title Right Now, No Title Ever!

Arrived by police car
& arrived by metaphor

France kept my wallet
& France ate my lunch

The snow is little swastikas
& the snow is tiny invoices

Did Beckett have a dog?

My Own History of the War

Pain drifted down the Ebro, landscape
was nice, stretched
like a painter on his easel. Mindless
was how the bullets
travelled, a new concept
where civilization flipped onto its belly. A major
loudmouthed history, nailed in a house
with no one to hear, but them
that grew tails, wrote songs
in praise of cigarettes, sense
saw where we were headed, decamped
& snuck off with the unusually swollen
we found wedged
between two hills. Honest.

Colonel Suasion, linear as ever,
advanced to the general command
of gibbons & macaws
with stripes that stood for limbs.

Sense drifted up the Ebro, wagging at those who knew,
blazed with the permanence of blood
on a flag round a corpse
over a grave, within a multitude
leaning over from the vertical
like a tree that lay down for one
tree second, out of which I grew
& was a teen, afraid, grew
& was an adult, afraid, then shrunk
into a dot that people said nice things
about, yeah, I wish
but a dot that mattered
until it failed to stop a sentence.

The general floated down the Ebro, drunk
on consonants, never caused a word
to be lost that he did not crow about
in his third or fourth
stab at an autobiography.

The general's body floated down the Ebro
then swole up & became children
of those who disappeared.

Meanwhile, below the river Ebro
or anywhere, one arm met another,
ran into a midsection
who knew where you could get a couple of legs,
cheap, &,
before you know it,
they met every Thursday
till they were a body...

And the body, my body, floats up & down the Ebro.

& the body fetches up right over there
where I said I love you once
to Leon Trotsky,
my dear Leon Trotsky,
I meant to *viajar contigo* to Mexico
but I had to float down that damn river
just one more time
& you left, my lovely Leon
& where you went
was not here
where I still float
in love with 1937.

We Are Berias

You remember revolutionizing hurricanes waiting for elevators,
stalking Lenin through Thishurtsyouworsethanmeya Street, pink
blood of the White Army bubbling up from the last copy of *The
Worker*, you wrote every article, bought every copy, toppled every
dragoon of the Tzarinistovich's forces; you held the hand of the small
child you forced to buy the ice pick, you packed the little bastard in a
crate, you shipped him off to Mexico, wrote him seven times in seven
days asking for a report, a word, a crumb, you ate your ticket out
because the ink was blueberry juice & you were starving, his letter
finally came to you, his bold lie of justice, his folds uneven & words
dripping over like Diego's moustache; you read that he had used the
pick, he's happy to tell you there is an empty chair at the café, one
less ogler of Rivera's hairy wife, one less chair at the table, you are
happy, yes, you are hungry, you look up with tears in your eyes that
are pink, there has never been a revolution, they had just invented
the elevator, 9,000 non-persons pulling on a rope & pulley to lift
your tiny spirit, you see a ray of light over the smudgepot horizon,
you know it is that fucker Mayakovsky, you write him a note that says
you will stand down, comrade, & die when I ask, you take the entire
nation of smells & farts & cabbagemen & snot & you realize you are
pregnant, little Josef in your belly like a sour immaculate conception.

97 Lines

for Nicanor Parra on the occasion of his 97th birthday, September 5, 2011

Can't walk
I am stone
the stone alone
this tossed aside by god
run over, shard of day
thin and nameless
a mere dustbunny of memory
become priest confessor
in this oubliette, this capillary
of group ignorance.
*

Someone confessed to me
distracted, punch-drunk
short by a hair, crumpled
and unheeding of the shit that happens to, say, you.
Zero, right
the shape of either a man's knee or the moon
that's an old man's knee, a shrink's moon
I've had the same eyes for these many hard years
they're gonna be my sugar-plum some night, baby
used, good for spotting movement, like a dog's.
**

Hey, rube
before you enter the tent
preferably through an entrance
linger a decade, consider the ant
does it toil or spin? What antly ambitions. What eight-footed lusts
echo through time to bring down an emperor
emperors, yeah, the modern goat

who carries his own desert within...
yeah, no one like me
scared painless.
***

Chickie and Bif Daddy
are so pissed their tongues flap
at me singing myself.
Adorable fine artist
born 1951
from crazy folk, noisy
until I clammed up
held my voice prisoner in my beard
shot the fucking parrot of self
guys and dolls.
****

Unsure quantum of fleshiness
one snowy mother
upright in a chair.
Dreaming a meal
absent
when the hell is lunch
a red chair is in love with me
unable to pose as a woman
waiting a lifetime
false promise! No kids, never.
*****

I haven't even started,
lockjawed, powered down
in a garden full of priests
the forest in my safe deposit box
it isn't talking either
one ticket to the realm
better make it an *aller-retour*

I'll come back as a dog
barking like a paladin
to improve this century!
******

Okeydokey with me
this plague of Santiagan monkeys
it's merely Eugenio, whom I'd believe
lads
whether I wanted to or not
but for the passage of time
but for the spiritual fortune squandered on mere spirit
fading backwards
in the city in which he lives or does not
& all his young.
****

& here's Paco Empieza, a character
a diversion
so many years
as Santiago, a city
till the earth turned sideways
& dumped him into the story as man
not the best ending
first to admit, but
hold your burros, *aburridos*
this cat has been fucked by the years.
****

Up late again
naked under some clothes
I have a season I need to show the doctor.

Too much time alone
dries your eyes
better than night, sleep

& what may lie below
I'm not translating that
flat out
think of me what you will.
****

Tensed verb
sick doctor
got here by fasting
solo
I am what you love about bread
I can see
round corners.

Gimmicks Penguin

after Ron Padgett

Pieces of penguin
covered in ideas like bloodspots on a shaved face.
Penguins explode above 38 Celsius
& the class don't got no thermometers,
so I draw a penguin on the blackboard,
a penguin that has seen the best minds of its generation
—I'll never tell you how they smell—
you'll never know who set off the penguin.
So why do penguins matter?
Because we have no space program.
Because there is one fat man in a bar
dreaming his next book will make him sexy, while
I sit there in the dark (it is cool,
cool enough for a penguin) while
I remember Dick and Jane, and,
oh yeah, Spot the Penguin.

Small Rocket Ship Spinning Atoms Logo

for Judy Merril

That's no meteor, that's a stone thrown
from the moon
by time-travelling Russian impersonators!
God, we're a single nuclear winter
from jellyfish riding our spines
through a theocratic purge!

Judy, I just found my first machine intelligence
stuck to flypaper in our outhouse.
It claims it is Booth Tarkington, destroyer of worlds!

The Saddest Story I Can Think Of

bp turned 66 today. He had several root canals at 61, in the worst
year ever for his teeth. During a dry period of almost six months, he
taught himself to cook vindaloo and worked in a restaurant in Little
India near my house. Ten years ago, a bunch of ambitious young
people expelled him from Coach House Press, and he self-published
the *Martyrology* Books 32 through 51. The biopsy of the mole was a
scare for some, but he pulled through. The resulting hair loss was
a scare for others, but his Pulp Press novel about it sold almost a
thousand copies. He had terrible luck throughout the '90s with the
hand-painted bikes, but the police returned at least two, albeit the
worse for wear and most of the words sanded off. We all remember
when he broke his leg dancing in rehearsal for the second *Fraggle
Rock* movie, and the botch I made of it as his stand-in. Few beyond
Ellie know about the several close calls he had during the 2005 trip
to Europe, although he did write about the incident at the British
Museum. Remember when last year he sang from Christmas to
New Years?

& Ten Lines for Sara Gonzalez

con un beso

Was the revolution like a butterfly?

I will braid the left side of my beard the day you go.

Who will look north for me?

Who will sing of the waves of pacifists swimming south?

Who will be the first among equals?

Who the queen of our going-away party, Hotel Marazul, Managua, July 25, 1987?

The cassette tape of history has faded.

Fascists are in the ascendant.

My heart is a fortress for a beautiful butterfly

made of razor & rainbow.

Northrop Frye, David W. McFadden and My Mother All Agree on One Thing

Mom put it best: "Jimmie, you've read so many books, you should just be able to put together bits and pieces into your own." Nothing thrilled Neruda more than sneaking a figurehead out of a friend's apartment and adding it to his collection. I just dreamed of a red dog eating mashed potatoes. If it had been a red wheelbarrow, perhaps my mother and William Carlos Williams could have finished their shift in this poem, and maybe gone out for a coffee, and soon after fallen in love. I declare her my most precious figurehead. Sure hope Neruda doesn't learn there is no lock on the back door of this poem. Please don't tell him, he may carry Mom off to Isla Negra where she would be happy. Perhaps you disapprove, think this is a godawful way to treat my mom. She had a life, and it ended, so there you have it. But there is so much loneliness in this world, if it were mashed potatoes, every dog in the joint would burst.

Non-stories

Non-story 1

I fell in love with Oubliette at the height of the Inquisition. It was not
meant to be. She was scheduled to be burned at sunrise, while I had
two full days left on the rack.

My last comfort was that we would have made such a pretty couple.
Her all smoky and me seven feet tall.

Kids? Hard to say.

Non-story 2

There is a 20% chance of Spanish Civil War today.
I turn right as I leave the house.
I push George Orwell into the gutter, seizing his umbrella.
I attend church.
I attend church.
Then I remember to close the umbrella.
Manna rains down upon me.
Buses drive over nuns
—Christ you never see nuns out & about anymore—
water cascades along the street & into sewers
filled with gold teeth & shorn hair.

Non-story 3

I walked in a mall, and no one noticed me. I spotted J.D., a name from high school, and he looked at me sideways. We talked about the need to be a pariah. Tried to help nail a calendar to the wall, but it kept falling.

Outside a solar flare baked off half the planet.

Non-story 4

What if only part of you got anorexic? Say your ass started shrinking, the flesh drying up, hipbones clattering on wooden chairs. Say you woke from your nap with the dog gnawing on your femur. Your dream of a prosthetic sandbagged by a downturn in the ecomony [sic], you rent your feet out for soup. The heat feels so nice. At first you are content to sit on the edge of the bowl. But you know one day you'll just slide on in. One day you do.

Non-story 5

Robert Heinlein gave Judy Merril a huge lecture on why he would not lend her 200 dollars to buy into a collective fallout shelter. It is 1963 in Milford, Pennsylvania. Outside town, a starving coyote eats a half sandwich thrown out a car window by Isaac Asimov. Distracted by the meal, the coyote does not see the steaming remains of a very small space ship, crushed under a tire. The first law of 1963 is to kill the president. I wished I had noticed, but I am sick at home on the couch reading a story by William Tenn about tiny aliens. Heinlein buys me chips, but I ignore them.

Non-story 6

Malaga: there are no straight lines when fleeing. We made our way to
France as we could.

Suddenly, five odd jaywalkers, each with a leg and a crutch. One
fell. We got out. Stukas dived, streams of shell casings wisping away
like smoke.

Go drag the fucking body off the road, I screamed.

Non-story 7

Monday, the earthquake made me finish the horror book sooner.
Tuesday, I read till my eyes bled. Wednesday, I discovered that if I
thought of you, you immediately phoned me. Thursday, a guy in the
subway, Raul Zurita's small plane and an Akita at Cherry Beach told
me the same joke. Friday, I chose to deflate like a gasbag. Saturday,
you grew younger after lunch. Sunday, I never woke up.

Non-story 8

The pitch is this. Raymond Radiguet did not die of typhoid in 1923.
He just went silent. Returned as Mike, the computer intelligence
who led a surprisingly successful lunar revolution against tyrannical
Earth in Heinlein's *The Moon Is a Harsh Mistress*. At the end of the
book, he goes silent & we all think he is dead. But he comes back. It
is the '70s, and he is a big bag of cocaine in the door panel of a car in
The French Connection. He goes silent again. Comes back as a bag of
chips in a vending machine. Goes silent. Comes back as "Non-story
8". This is quite autobiographical.

Non-story 9

From where I sit, Bella could be spontaneously combusting downstairs. My office could be spontaneously combusting. Three hitmen in wheelchairs could be rolling down the street with a greasy old photo of me to guide them. The chair I always sit in in the kitchen could be passing the Turing test. France could have a change of mind. Tom Thomson could be crawling along the bottom of a lake, telling himself goddammit only 30 more years and I'm outta here. My only comment on nature: twigs all look alike, and as for fucking snow, it's identical.

Non-story 10

A dog walks into a vet's office. Am I here yet, he asks the slab of wall. I am sitting in a chair with George Orwell. I ask George if we should answer the dog. He says no, I think the dog is doing just fine. The wall is silent. The dog continues to stare at the wall. Outside cars rust, saxifrage breaks through the sidewalk. The dog continues to stare at the wall. "Call Me Ishmael" by the Chi-Lites is playing through the speaker system. When the song ends, the dog walks out of the vet's office.

Last Non-story

"Seventeen fucking years crossing America putting those microdot bibles* in every room. Every single one handwritten. You can shove the job up your ass, that's what you can do."

*Microdot Bible (actual size)   ●

Curious Things I Wore

Bandages on each of my ten fingers to a restaurant.[1]
Rodents.
Purple crushed velvet waist-length jacket with a high Elvis collar.[2]
The Cape Breton coastline.
A wet face cloth on my head in Managua.[3]
An economic summit.
My sister's nylons.[4]
Fruitcake.
A helmet of blood.[5]
The first law of robotics.

1. A teacher had asked the "brains" out to a restaurant to celebrate our loneliness, or something. I had never been to one, and the bandages were to provide plausible deniability for any *faux pas* I might commit.
2. I had bought it, a canary-yellow short leather jacket, and some ruffled shirts from Kingston's first head shop. I wore it riding my one-speed bicycle, sitting bolt upright and smoking Cameos on the way to a university class.
3. In front of 100,000 Nicaraguans and nine *comandantes*, in the international delegation area on the 10th anniversary of the revolution, because it was hot.
4. It was cold and I had no plans to take my pants off.
5. Stood straight up into a girder for Conklin Shows, my ex drove me to emergency, a road repair signalman peered into the Volkswagen and fainted.

Excellent Coffee of Chalatenango

The cup of coffee spoke.
I drank blood from the time I was a seedling.
They fertilized me with red leftist flesh and brass bullet casings.
Those who picked me were killed on the spot.
I was roasted on a bed of their bones.
I was shipped here across slave galley routes.
You sit where the poor used to live.
Have the mercury sandwich.
It is fresh every day.

Milton

Looked for you in last week no luck, sure weren't in that last note from Clifford, & China says their manned exploration program will not be there to search for you till 2020. Then I read in the paper that you washed up on the shore of Ireland, the note inside still legible, when I tuned in the shortwave you snored between stations. Come back, Milton, all is forgiven, in this dimension Mark Strand never left PEI, just rambles on endlessly about how he could write a book to every mother who says that boy is much too good-looking to work at OLCO, a wholly owned subsidiary. You coulda punched him to next Tuesday.

Things I've Died from Recently

Running away from bears.
Running toward bears.
Failing to look at a diabetic's feet
carefully when they are my own.
Getting angry & holding
my breath while swallowing my tongue.
Inhaling food
reading too much
reading not enough
falling
asleep while angry.

Things I Died from in the Past

Running off a cliff on the Cabot Trail.
Going with Jimmy Murtagh to take that first hit of speed.
Not being recognized at 4 a.m. by the asshole with a sawed-off .22.
Drowning on the way home while blacked out.
My dad's two-pound hammer.
Pounding bullets with a rock.

Things I Will Die from Eventually

Failure to ever get to the moon.

Thou, Refusenik

after Vladimir Mayakovsky

Yikes, brother! Gromyko's obit was bang on.
By morning Mezcalin's cenotaph had aged.
Art thou the enemy? Thy musselman's tenderness
Makes heaven carve its mansion into apartments,
Breed robots, our constitutional undergrowth.
Andreyevich only mocked personalism in others,
But took out his own teeth. He was my enemy nonetheless,
Bunkered behemoth, third in order.

Thou, refusenik, come to my death humbly:
Today Orlovsky heaved the Comintern office over one shoulder,
Was reported an 11 a.m. sensation,
Smothered in self-criticism by evening,
& joined me in this pit by midnight.

1930. The year I enlisted in the army of the dead.

Poets of the 20th: Research Poem for Ed Sanders

bpNichol at 44 of sudden blood loss during an operation
Roque Dalton at 45 shot by members of his own party
Gwendolyn MacEwen at 46 of alcoholism
Vladimir Mayakovsky at 36 of self-inflicted gunshot
Federico García Lorca at 38 beaten to death by francoist thugs outside
      Granada his hometown
Hilda Doolittle at 75 by stroke
Jack Spicer at 40 of alcoholism
Leonel Rugama at 20 in a post bank robbery siege by the National Guard
Muriel Rukeyser at 66 by stroke
Daniel Jones at 35 by his own choice
Ted Berrigan at 49 of complications from a life of speed
Sylvia Plath at 30 by her own choice
Paul Éluard at 56 of heart attack
Ed Dorn at 70 of cancer of the pancreas
Gabriela Mistral at 67 of cancer of the pancreas
Charles Baudelaire at 46 of stroke and paralysis
Gregory Corso at 70 of cancer of the prostate
Lorine Niedecker at 67 of cerebral hemorrhage
Pablo Neruda at 69 of heart failure from cancer of the prostate
Joe Brainard at 52 from pneumonia from AIDS
Marianne Moore at 84 by stroke
Arthur Rimbaud at 37 of cancer of the leg
Frank O'Hara at 40 from a ruptured spleen after being hit by a dune buggy
Denise Levertov at 74 by complications from lymphoma
David Aylward at 46 by choice

Use the space below to record your observations
Add sheets as needed

Bear Attacks

The day before
the data.
A week later
the wardens shot & killed him.

I was scheduled
to forage in campgrounds
success with shouting
but only experts.

Sidearms have
black and grizzly
behaviour.

You are the park
you can often buy time
with garbage.

A small boulder
fishing in several creeks
survived.

Horses camp.
Dogs shout.
Management & scats
are hard to tell apart.

Near a carcass
it is impossible to be precise.

I used to fear
existence, who could
handle the recoil?

This book
hit me with its paw
my mouth
assumed many different positions.

Where did I feed
when. Odours
be alert!

To Whom Must I Complain

You woke me & I found woodchucks
scribbling laws all over my *tabula rasa*.
You woke me & that day
no one sued me for breathing, but
I got a ticket for eating commas.
Small clouds shaped like a punch from George Chuvalo
sucked droplets from the garden, & I found a hat
to protect my genitals, which I typed as gentles.
May I humbly suggest you just bugger off with your
aphoristic kleptomania?

The Instrumentality of Dogs

for Anne Waldman

I

A dog just ran across Pont Neuf. Two guys, Shirtfull and Shirtless, ignore the dog, pointedly. The Museum of Modern Art sinks beneath something awfully white. Shirtfull whispers to a tree: The Nelson Atkins Museum shall become a pound, for people, if I were king.

II

One staircase, not a soul in sight. Crooked tree, a single arcteryx surveilling. Nothing to see here, river, move on. The purple of that wall, the chiaroscuro-iness of one fat painting, facedown on the bank. Where did Pound go? Into his cantos? It is a mere 3,827 miles to Saint Elizabeth's.

III

When we were human, I touched a dwarf. 53 years later I saw three across the street from Les Deux Magots, & suddenly embarrassed, yearned to go back to assure the first dwarf I meant no diminishment, how could I, the thing within my robe, being me, sought to be at one with another, thought an extended hand (the right) would suffice. Now there is no proof. Just this royal clusterfuck. So close to the Sorbonne.

IV

Pablo & Salvador dressed up like medieval burghers.
You're going to have to define this more.

V

I finally meet the ghost crab. We stare. We stand on a salt flat at the
end of the universe, near the community centre. He is so there in the
moment. I question why I am always attracted to *gravitas*.

VI

Take that *favela*. Pile it on another. And another. Pile a dozen on top.
Let sit for 300 years. Darkness lies between. Look, there, at the heart,
beneath the pile of *favelas*, shining out of darkness, a golden palace.
There is so much light, it must belong to a luminescent prince. The
envy. The self-loathing. I am ashamed of my *favela* upbringing, my
ghost crab, my personal reference, my victimhood at the stubby
hands of dwarves, my lifelong worship of Pound so jejune it would fit
on a postcard from France.

The Fate of Chile

I know what happened to Jara,
but where is Luis Navarro now?
I know what happened to Allende,
but the fate of Sam Rojas is unclear to me.
Jara and Allende are safe
in history, but Luis and Sam
may still be having a tough time.
Or a great time.
The wooden ship of curiosity
runs aground on my shore, my natives are
butchered, my golden thoughts are
plundered, a class system is established
throughout my body.
Friends I never would have had
but for Pinochet,
friends I never would have lost
but for Pinochet.
Never would have read Parra
but for Pinochet.
Never would have envied Tellez
but for Pinochet.
This should be called "Thank You, Pinochet"
but just can't do it.

Cento for O'Hara

The cinema is cruel!
The earth is everywhere!
Christ, I worry a lot about becoming a mere
me, a madness in the forest,
a widow!
Look at the clouds a minute!
We so seldom look on love!
And the gods who don't live there!
Maybe I won't go to sleep at all
in 1951! Maybe
it would like to think!
No more dying!
I think I have started to fall!
And now at last I am
a mutter and a faint trace of pain!

Corn Gun

Yellow bullets grow &
inevitably, a corn gun!
Single shot, then
full cob firing, soon
exploding cobs, cob mines &
multi-cob launchers, compete
for distance &
whole fields raining down!
No surprise the corn atom's
weaponized & thereafter exponentialized,
blast equivalent of 100 cobs, 1 million cobs,
too soon a tera-cob device &
too soon, way
too soon, the cob to end all cobs.

What They Think of Dave McFadden

for Merlin Homer

Ed Sanders felt David was overshadowed by events at Columbia.
Charles Olson remembered that he held the flute he played with
      serpent arms.
Pound wrote to Mencken that "he has right."
Whitman valued the wonder everyone sees in everyone else he sees.

Charles Simic accused Dave of torturing him every day.
Mayakovsky saw him on Pushkino's foothill, humpbacked with Akulova.
Spicer merely stated that to Dave the sun is beautiful.
Parra knew Dave could offend the armed forces, and said so.

Aleksandr Skidan once saw him glistening in the darkness like an
      open mollusk.
Bolaño, by contrast, thought of him as an enormous drugged bird.
Brautigan stared out the window and saw him.
Williams asked Dave to forgive him because they were delicious, so
      sweet and so cold.

Di Prima found him as one of two men a wolf between them.
Burroughs saw Dave as variations.
O'Hara once told him that dawn must always recur.
Padgett admired him because he knew what acrostics were.

Guernica 1

Bombings are all the same.

Spanish has seven different words for dust. The dust of buildings,
the dust of bodies, & the dust of mixed bodies & buildings. The dust
of plants & animals, the dust of toys, the dust of paper & ideas, & the
dust that settles over history.

I have a ticket for Guernica I will never use. Dropped into my
mailbox, no return address, no stamp, no envelope & content
missing.

There is math to bombing.
There is artistry to bombing.
There is pure bombingness to bombing.

Guernica 2

Bomb the Geek Squad Smart Car
Bomb the vowel "e"
Bomb the stock boy at Loblaws in 1967
Bomb Facebook
Bomb my grade 12 math teacher Mr. Chisamore
Bomb malice, our nickname for our apple tree,
& bomb the raccoons.

Bomb Harper's lair
Bomb the Mare of Toronto
Bomb Lake Ontario
Bomb the last copy of *Beowulf*
Bomb the 700 block of Division Street in Kingston
& bomb my left back pocket.

Bomb every book from Delacorte
Bomb every word that crawls away
Bomb Downton Abbey a purely fictional place
Bomb Camus' car on that sandy road
& bomb that tulip farthest from my window.

Bomb the orphanage
Bomb the space shuttle
Bomb the very petal as it grows
& bomb the Spanish language.

Bomb him.
Bomb her.
Bomb the whole lot.
Bomb what's left
Bomb what could never be
& finally, please, bomb me.

Guernica 3

Bomb 1 (shoelaces) fell straight through the Earth.

Bomb 3 (nun's habits) had ears like a carrot.

Bomb 5 (feathers) fell on bomb 31.

Bomb 7 (milk) suffered from Minamata disease.

Bomb 11 (small licorice swastikas) sent a truck careening into
       Stephen King in 2002.

Bomb 17 (sigils pointing up) became dizzy.

Bomb 19 (infant's breath) found a footstool made from an elephant's leg.

Bomb 23 (heart attacks) ceased to exist.

Bomb 29 (kittens) drowned Tom Thomson.

Bomb 31 (a thousand acts of contrition) voted.

Bomb 37 (hair clippings) was from Texas.

Bomb 41 (kisses) spanked the mayor.

Bomb 43 (garlic) spoke French with an aluminum accent.

Bomb 47 (pictures of machine-gun bullets) landed smack-dab in the
       middle of the Last Supper.

Guernica 4

Interim Inventory:

247 extra buildings.
120 extra animals.
7 extra priests.
3 extra libraries.
42 extra laneways.
4 extra plazas.
701 extra men.
412 extra women.
187 extra children.

12 Prayers for Romero

Identify yourself.
Cover yourself.
For godsake
cease the repression.
It is 2012 and I
am an answer on *Jeopardy*.
Alex Trebek lies buried
under the floorboards.
His mother was a Carmelite,
his daddy was big Roberto D'Aubuisson.
Villagers walk through the army camp,
choose random colonels
for promotion.
Next Tuesday we'll pray
for a clean head shot.

Experiment to Demonstrate the Pact of Forgetting

for Judge Baltasar Garzón of Spain

Purpose

> Identify what is down there.

Equipment

> Rondo, a town.
> A long rope.
> A notebook.
> A pen.
> A shovel.
> A flashlight.

Method

> 1. Tie rope to something sturdy.
> 2. Descend steep cliff into ravine using rope.
> 3. Use shovel to dig down to 1937.
> 4. Use flashlight to see.
> 5. Use notebook to record entries.

Observations

> 1. It is hard to go down a ravine using a rope.
> 2. You have to dig a bit to get to 1937.
> 3. Everything is all mixed up & jumbled together.
> 4. Often you cannot identify anyone.
> 5. Sometimes you can, with varying degrees of certainty.

Conclusions

1. There are a lot of people down there.
2. It is sometimes possible to determine if someone was a Republican or a fascist rebel.
3. Those identified were:
    a. Jesus Christ of Nazareth
    b. Leon Trotsky
    c. Betty Boop
    d. Myself
    e. Grendl
    f. 4 wolfmen
    g. Frank Sinatra
    h. Kiki
    i. Fatty Arbuckle &
    j. The current King.

At the Lenox Montparnasse Room 37

André Breton entered me through the nose. I sneezed on the
Communist Manifesto.

Marcel Duchamp hung round my eye until I was not looking,
dived in and pulled the lid over himself. I can feel him doing the
breast stroke.

Kiki pulled my pants down and made me pose for Man Ray when
I was not ready, or dressed. She called that *Sex in Montparnasse*.
I have ever since been too shy to dine at Le Dome.

Di Chirico erased my features and convinced me to be a cone. I stand
a lot.

But Éluard, he was the one. He gathered them all into this greyish
photo, in which they stare transfixed, hoping I shall blink, spare
them the bleak view, the bleak, bleak view of you.

Loon Sky Lake Shore Fish

1

There is a loon.
There is a sky.
There is a loon.
There is a lake.
There is a loon.
There is a shore.
There is a fish.
Each touches the other along one plane.

2

Actually, there are three loons: loon 1, loon 2 and newborn loon .5.
The family unit of 2.5 travel together. They make noise. They eat,
they shit, they move about in the water. They disappear.

3

The lake is pure information. Loon .5 floats on it, through the air,
pure sensation. Loons 1 and 2 float through the lake. They turn
downwards, they dive, disappear into the lake of information.

4

Last week loon .5 made faint noises when 1 and 2 disappeared. This
week .5 ducks his head into the information. He sees 1 and 2, but
they are different. Immersion in information has changed them. He
raises his head out of the lake and makes a noise. He says, "Blert!"

5

Every time .5 puts his head into the lake, something lies to him. I am fish, I am your friend. I am water, there is nothing to know.

6

Loon 1 breaks surface with a small fish in her mouth. I am not to be eaten, says the small fish. I shall destroy you and all whom you care for. I shall call on the big fish god to come and save me. Loon 1 gives the small fish to .5, who swallows the fish whole. Shall I suffer, .5 asks loon 2, which has surfaced with a small fish in his mouth. I saw what you did and I will tell on you, says the small fish. I will tell the sky.
.5 swallows loon 2's gift.

7

.5 eventually has a stomach full of threats, he is to be killed, told upon, lied about and taken from this place to a place of nothingness. Something squirts out of him. He is worried that it is his life. But he is still floating on the surface. He ducks his head into the lake of information.

8

Fish 5 sees the whitish swirl that drifts down and recognizes 1 through 4. Fish 5 is appalled, or haunted, and starts to warn fish 6. Loon 2 collects fish 5 in its beak and breaks for the surface. Loon 1 and loon 2 move off into the weeds at the north edge of the lake. The weeds are Man's Work, which has grown through information into sensation.
.5 cannot see them.

9

.5 grows.

10

The lake contains every song that has ever been sung. It contains the
music of every century.

Do and Die

Lorca stood in the angry doorway. It has nothing to do with me. Stay away from my poems, or I will kill you. I wait on a bridge just outside Granada. I drop a five-ton Acme anvil on him, but forget to let go the rope attached to the anvil, so I am pulled off after the anvil, exude a puff of cloud and speed lines as I fall, cannot remember whether I or the anvil will hit Lorca first. The rope is *duende*.

I Am Not a List

I am not the president, an onion ring, a fried ant, noxious, truncated
or emergent.
I am not Fred, Barney, Jimmy Olsen, Auntie Em, William Carlos
Williams, or a tree.
I am not outside digging my way out of a jail cell and happy during
earthquakes.
I am not a pissant, a threnody or gluten-free.
I am not glowing in this dimension, awaiting scientific proof, or
living rolled up like a building plan.
I am not Hindenburgian, Titanickish, or a citizen of Dresden.
I am not a barrel of herring, a cretin, or without tentacles to rely upon.
I am not a password, a brackish pond, or *excrementa*.
I am not the Pope.
I am not wild in the streets, a billionaire, or tumescent.
I am not a Glock, a Fassbinder, a Sapphic oracle or last year's
hornet nest.
I am not a nice guy, a stream of piss, Tuesday's *Star*, that blurry
Doberman in *The Omen*, or nude.
I am not this theorem, that nebula, or the other tanning salon.
I am not my last pair of Florsheims, a dune buggy, or cholesterol.
I am not Daisy Zamora's car, St. Elmo's fire, or Toronto in flames.
I am not capable, warm, or built.
I am not the world in quotes, a parenthetical chigger, or capable
of negation.
I am not this page.

Parliamentary Suite

Gag Reflex

Because 300 poets killed themselves, because a french child
assembled a passable Leon Trotsky from Lego, because a bird
pecked out my left eye, because I saw bpNichol at Woodbine slots
(he was winning), because I am a pitbull full of love & teeth, because
nothing works, because Superman exists only by consensus, because
the first six prime numbers are 1, 2, 3, 5, 7 & 11 but then it gets dicey,
because Liz Toroni's acid made the sky wriggle, because Parliament
is an infection.

Parliamentary Suite (continued)

From the Secret Diary of Parliament

For some time I had been seeing weird shit.
My stomach felt like something walking.
Several questions blocked the door when I tried to leave.
They would let me out sometimes at night
as long as I did not wear a shirt
so I would blend in with the moon.
Walking, I would think of Attila
and politics.
Days, poetry took up all the space
which made me too self-conscious
so I was glad to blend in with the moon.
Somewhere between two tables in a bar
a sound whimpered it was an emergency
but that was the very moment a speech
beat another speech to death with a stick.
Surely you heard about that.
Thus precious moments were lost
while my party got a tattoo
it called doubt
on its tiny little religious doubt.
You can take precautions, sure,
but reason never sails a ship straight,
not even when plants keep their heads down
in a tall, tall world.
Of course I got mugged for my worst presentiments,
the telephones stopped ringing
and littered the ground I walked on.
My trembling hand wrote a wrong number
only good when I slept.
Uncertainty placed second at the polls,
waiting for a foreign sound

to stab it with a pencil.
Meanwhile, down the arroyo,
the dentists of Belsen
fell from the sky, hoping their passports
could be renewed, black
as the back of your eye.
I offered my tongue up as a roast
for the sake of some conversation.
I was so fucking tired
of batteries. Electricity
had to make a comeback.
I need to share my worry about questions.
Erotic self-censure failed me
and I ended up hungry.

Bad jokes consume time a landlady just doesn't have.
Stupid talk beneath a convulsing sky
is not the Soul-Destroyer
it is just stupid talk beneath the convulsing sky.
I compliment you
on my imprisonment—
usually I'd hate it,
but since tomorrow
I'll forget the church again, anyway,
thanks.

After "La Trampa" by Nicanor Parra

Parliamentary Suite (concluded)

Call Me Agonistes

for Stephen "The Butcher" Harper

I looked for the initials I had carved in my nose as a child.
In their place was a tiny tv screen.
It had only one channel, a loop of a single mosquito landing.
There was nothing I could do.

When I held the mirror just so, I could see the back of my head,
and if I parted my hair just right, I could see another tv,
showing what was in front of my face,
which if I have this right, made my head invisible.

Self-examination showed me there were several in my groin,
currently off the air, but I worried what they showed to whom
and if the light from their tiny screens bled through my underpants.
I lay down to worry.

I watched my feet screens
show me walking straight away toward the horizon,
complete with clouds of gnat-like citizenry
cheering me on in gnat-like voices.

Pumpkin Centigrade

It's not about us.
It's not about what the dog smelled.
It's not even about adjectives.

It's not about anything cantilevered.
It's not about a poet in residence.
It's not even about the cold and lonely drive to Sunday.

It's not about my favourite smell.
It's not about the two clowns pissing barcodes.
It's not about a half bag of stale elegies.

It's full of doughnuts.
It won last night on *Jeopardy*.
It kissed me goodbye in French.

It's not about my underarm hair.
It's not about a building's footprint.
It's not about the speck of light in the sky tonight.

It's not about you.
It's not about some finger floating in the dark.
It's not even about pumpkin centigrade, after all.

John Milton

for Michael Fleishman

Of this wheelchair, nothing, but my heart could stop
on a dime, each friend a home run, &
my baritone still moves among
the stars. Legally, I built an empire
of friends, plaintiffs, artists, my acquaintance
so crowded you couldn't swing a wheelchair.

My family became my family, remember
my little dog, we cried about the
shortness & the quick steps of his life.

Christt, Elqui

2

By February 5, 1927
I caught myself working
my way north with an Albanian.
Just following orders
North American style
stealing the silver
for those who'd come after!
It was a pissy situation
stretched across a bed
drunk blind or both
and then I hear my name
from up above
so I freeze, see,
blood cowers in my vein
while it got so hot
my pants expanded
I thought it was all over
so may as well stop lying
stop making people stupid.
An old god spoke me, &
my eyes flopped out on this sidewalk
so surprised they started frying
desperate I did pushups
made myself a telegram
to myself about getting smarter
there was a stone in my eye
the size of a kid
forgot I was a man
who did things right.

4*

Pinochet caused a bible to be buried with Neruda. Every year
he would have the grave dug up, and every year the bible had
transformed into some other book. One year Pound's *Cantos*, the
next a peasant's cookbook. Quickly enough, the former bibles filled
an entire shelf. Pinochet started burying other books, bad books, in
the hope they would turn into bibles. They did not. When I heard
this story, I immediately wrote to Pinochet and asked that he bury
himself. My answer was a whipping in the square of Iquique. My
hope was that he would eventually have to turn into Neruda.

4.1

Each dream a jewel
unaffordably tactile
priceless & nourished
by the wind of my chapbooks
which numbered several thousand
each in a hotel-room desk drawer
I travel just to autograph them
an indecipherable scrawl
!

5

One stop beatification
lose the beard
your will is enough
to force yourself up from underground.
Didn't even break a sweat
the enemy fell back

empty-handed
hoping I would be pissed
at all the kneeling marks
but it's what I told you, sweetheart
if virtue's all it's cracked up to be
then no one, absolutely no
one would suffer
out of order.
Wait your turn!

6

Practical character advice?
Don't sleep in
eat red things in daylight
& wash them down
until your shoes stretch.
No calcium if bare-headed
be meat weekly
be vegetable rarely
never eat in your shell
it's all poison!
If you must kill a parrot
don't.
Wash out the holy urinals
after breakfast.
Nap for milliseconds
never past the point of unconsciousness
never sleep with a bad person.
Burp
to save your tripe.
Never fuck Holy Week
but if you must, wrap it up in 15 minutes.
Be white somewhere.
Hang on to your mother if deceased

but your pop can be buried.
Play a mean lute.
This one's personal, if it's scary
pass it on to an enemy
wear black
but not if you are outside.
Start making mistakes now,
in 20 years it's too late!

8

I'm more plant than magician.
I'm more diuretic than laxative.
I'm more demon than driver.
Resurrection's art's
A closed shop!

10*

When my mother stopped existing, the black lab she yearned to have
had took her confession in its drooly mouth & ran. As it was written,
as it shall be.

11

This just in!
The sooner you see god
the sooner your printer will seize up like a stone
editing will be done with switchblades
you'll be such a good Spaniard.
Yeah, I flung myself into the desert
so hard I bounced for seven years.
Thought I was the best,

abandoned my alphabet
couldn't tell a door from a ladder
rats ate my pope
who said some damn bad things.
Dear ones: now is the moment
reality is determined by he
with the biggest typewriter.
I can cross-dress as Christ
run out for smokes like a regular joe
make a fucking fetish of my humility
but please laugh when you read this
I was pregnant by love
by the attention you paid so dearly.

17

Hey! Hide the priests!
There's a huge rent in the sky &
something with painted cheeks
peeks through asking to be noticed!

18

Avoid the thousand-year dustup,
no fun fundamentalism
no plague plagiarism.
Be a friend of enemyism
dream something up on your own
dig it like a free thinker.
As they say in Santiago:
No sea bestia!

20

A cow attending a funeral of a tree.
How much for that priest in the window?
The one with the puppy dog's eyes?

23

No, Father, ya gotta sing!
Silence fails to persuade.
Don't worry about Augustine,
he's got no soul
no verbs.
His voice shall not be heard
by god, that artist
of the vocal chords.

33

Ready I'm not, got here as a child, gloves didn't fit, no beard believed
in me. How many years was I a card-carrying member of the Party of
No Fingernails? No matter. I'm here trailing my word balloon, shorn.
I want to talk to you about worship. I want to talk to you about not
fucking with anyone, despite my abject history of being fucked with.
Twenty years of fuckery, thirteen minutes to explain.

I am become naked.

The punishment of uniforms is over.

Risk Analysis of a Poem

There is a 49% chance this poem will not be finished.
There is a 7% chance it will veer off into prose.
About 7,000 words should be held in reserve until we see where this
is going.
We should be able to reduce that number when the chance of the
poem being finished drops below 25%.
There is a one in a million chance you will be named in this poem,
either as a major player, as a metaphor or as a noun.
Two dogs just ran through the preceding line.
There is now a 41% chance this poem will be finished, unless the
writer is eating.
There is an even chance this poem is being written in a workshop.
Now would be a good time to drop in a word in a foreign language.
C'est ça.
The prose possibility has dropped to near nil.
Will it be a successful poem?
There is a 5% chance it will appear in a magazine.
There is a 5% chance that someone will buy the magazine.
Now might be the best time to develop a theme.
C'est ça.
There is a definite lack of, I don't know, something, to here. But it
appears here, so that's fine.
We are back on track
and I am extremely happy to report that there are only several more
lines required for this to satisfy the writer.
There is a constant rainfall outside the window.
Ronald Reagan has just been shot in the unmentionables.
Ten million U.S. dollars were handed to a man from El Salvador who
cannot stop touching himself.
Gerard Manley Hopkins is about to write "The Windhover"
so that millions of schoolchildren have something to memorize.
There is zero chance they would memorize this poem,
because it lacks.
It lacks Camus at the wheel, it lacks the ability to be translated into French,

or, rather, it lacks the raw will to force itself into French unbidden.
The Salvadoran man has returned to his Salvadoran country and is
shooting Salvadorans.
That's damn tidy.
He will continue to shoot Salvadorans until this poem comes to an end.
Due to a stray bolt of empathy, a desire to cook supper and a dog's bark,
this poem has come to an end.
Please stop shooting Salvadorans, it is no longer the '80s.
Did Reagan die?
Stop, it's over, I implore you, an end to this poem means
at least one Salvadoran man will stop shooting Salvadorans.
Be a Saviour.
There's one in every box.

5 True Statements

The puddle of blood in the park looked like a happy face.

Mud is so hard to get off fiction.

When the moon is full, there's a little guy who does a dance.

My first rifle had a speech impediment.

At Cherry Beach I saw a copy of me float toward the spit.

The New Managua

for Arnie

I remember your tail wagging when you slept in French.
The lump on your side made out of chocolate.
How you panted during thunderstorms in space,
the two times we almost lost you to Cambridge
& that first seizure when you voted.
The blackness of your fur whenever I wore it, I miss
the blackness of your fur whenever I wore it.

The Airplane of Grief Crash-Lands
on the Runway of My Heart

Pepé Le Pew chose to die
for what Sylvester had tried to steal.
Poor Fudd said his his his stutter made him shy
from witnessing Wile E. Coyote's last meal.

Mr. Jetson was in fact conceived with no penis
because the jetmobile caused his mother to smother.
His testes fled to Venus
Where Jetson was cloned by his brother.

In truth the Roadrunner was never defeated,
though he has ached unfettered
in pursuit of rerun fame reheated
alas only watched by we unlettered.

Struth for years I grew up on pop
& chips from the nearest Quik-Stop.

The Death of José Robles*

The death of José Robles
weighed three and a half pounds at birth.
It covered half a city block
and there are no pictures.

The death of José Robles
owned nothing but a time machine,
two shoes
and a brick of cheese.

The death of José Robles
smoked, hid in beards,
licked itself nightly
and wanted to be pope.

The death of José Robles
met him one night off Las Ramblas,
seized his hand
and fell in love.

* Someone killed exiled Spaniard José Robles, a U.S. academic and Republican
sympathizer, early in the Spanish Civil War. Who did, and why, is controversial.
Hemingway's reaction to the death ended his friendship with John Dos Passos.

Life of All the Pirates in History

Eventually, the following day, then, the following morning, afterwards, the loot! Finally, for the next fourteen days, after this, again and again, he gave them a bottle of rum. When, then, of course, the first man to see a sail, less than half an hour later! For two years, at a little after two o'clock in the afternoon, now, once this was established, he received a ten percent share. Meanwhile, after which, if there had been more daylight left, at this point, not unnaturally, in the first place, so ended the prisoners. For the next few weeks, cat and mouse, he was led from the dock, once again, then, when, seeing an opportunity, all along the way, for two years, for two years, shortly thereafter, his thumbs were bound with cord, at dawn, they were hung and they were hanged as well.

Exit Interviews

1. Milton Acorn

for Mark Strand

I've tasted the wormcasts of Europe,
No direction I couldn't walk.
My heart's my love,
What I was born to.
I shout that he has hands,
I saw one with wings.
No direction I couldn't walk.
The heart's five-pound brain
Shouts fire was want.
The beast has no language.
Walk with me.
Shout with me.
Walk with me.
Shout with me.
[remain silent for one minute]

From various poems by Milton Acorn

2. Ted Berrigan

POOF!
I'm dead.
& you can't keep me here
as is mine
great mud intelligence,
that icebox I hadn't read.
You can't keep me—
Davy Crockett is right on
what thoughts I have
smoking a pipe
you can't keep.
Sober dog
white powder
Ron Padgett said
—me here—
go back to speed
Chicago,
it's made of everything!

from The Collected Poems of Ted Berrigan *(University of California Press,* *2005)*

3. Otto René Castillo

To the interrogation of fruit, flowers, bones.
I say heart, mornings, joy.
Little country of mine, blind, voiceless,
walk with me, mountains, sing,
invent hurricanes,
& know this, colonel:
when I burn,
only I burn.

from my translation of various poems by Otto René Castillo

4. Roque Dalton

I disagree!
With four Mondays a month
or nine years
it's not the heat
when you know I'm dead
my General,
the speakers at the seventh congress
have aged an awful lot
the writers have lice
socialism has lice
Cain & Abel have lice
hope has lice
so I'm bringing you this little drink of water &
a pencil stub &
anguish,
my name & the sea.

from Small Hours of the Night *(Curbstone Press, 1996)*

5. Ed Dorn

West, more west
way more west.

Impeccable honour
smug guns
a cut plain
cowboy!

Juana *amiga*
mission bells
civil rights!

Eyes like two bits
or woman, Lil
Mexican ground
not this
not that
pain. The body
I am, I love
these dogs,
Wayne Kimball
& the world: hands up!

from Way More West: New and Selected Poems *(Penguin Poets, 2007)*

6. Federico García Lorca

At five in the afternoon.
I will not see it.
Spain is the only country.
Yet the Milky Way
has filled the valleys of Spain.
The rest was death.
Now, archer, now
there are newly created things,
there are jellyfish,
there are angels who never attack.
I love the song
I love the cartwheel
I love the rooster.
Qué pasa, rooster?
The best bullfighters fall,
torn apart by the horns
of their mothers.
Spain stretches out
at five in the afternoon,
all is finished,
the bull
loses itself, the fighter
scares himself.

from In Search of Duende *(New Directions, 1998)*

7. Mayakovsky

People are battlefields.
Famine, a giant ship.
It's time to act.
It's time to act.
Where's your pen.
Cold sweat
of all the wars,
millions of peasants
like melons
with treacherous generals.
Lightning in a museum
most humane.
Invaded by boots.
The scrap heap of
Lenin will
stare at the posters
all day, buried alive
instinctively.

from Vladimir Ilyich Lenin *(Progress Publishers, 1976)*

8. Pablo Neruda

Neruda, caballo verde de la poesía

Neruda, they burned you
Neruda, they did not sail from the seaports
Neruda, stored in the darkness
Neruda, here comes the tree!
Consul to farmlands and beehives
Chronicler of the troops in tatters .
Lover of returning home in dreams
Deliverer of letters.
He wrote that in tyranny's dense purple cheese another worm
awakens.
He saw you writing on the night's interminable walls.
He threatened that those who murdered Miguel Hernández in the
prisons of Spain would pay.
He confessed his childhood was wet shoes and broken trunks.
Left his old books
Left his houses
Left the party
Singing beneath the clandestine wings of his country.
Miners, march like an army. Arrive like someone who lands on a
stone moon,
With a bottle of gas and a guitar in your hand.
How happy we are!

from Canto General, *trans. Jack Schmitt (University of California Press, 1991)*

9. bpNichol

Forgotten
shark brain
apparition diction
classical coherence
deaf stranger
zero
wanting
room.

I is holy
around you!

from gIFTS: The Martyrology Book(s) 7& *(Coach House Press, 1990)*

10. Frank O'Hara

Pan seized the reed, said
when I was a child
I played by myself. But
New York is everywhere,
lean quarterlies & swarthy periodicals,
so I go for a walk.
I went to my first movie &
we are all thinking of you.
I am sitting crying at the corner
I will say it, thank god, I knew you would,
partly because of
Kennebunkport, partly because of
your annual cocktail party, partly
because of I was usually lying.
So I go for a walk.
Park Avenue, *Daily Mirror*, Queen Flab—
we will never be rich, I want to die
unadorned—
Hello Frank O'Hara how are you!
So I go for a walk.
It's fun to run around
a million guys!
So I go for a walk.
I think you're
the fierce!

from The Collected Poems of Frank O'Hara *(University of California Press, 1995)*

II. Charles Olson

1963:
Of the city,
the dog's upper lip.
As of myself,
off-shore.
Love is not easy
it is undone business
is not the equal of the night sky,
Europe, Thursdays, the East African Rift—
Dogtown!

People want delivery.

Other men of the town,
occupying the yellow house, I,
I am the child,
my shore
takes marks & bears Junk!
Or we will leave her,
1966 full of sounds
on his side
vessels pass through
the night sky, Dogtown
is soft!
My arrogance
hath charge of the hold,
I count such shapes
enthusiasm.
I know I am
a house made of mud & wattles.
Nor is that all
which still is,
in other words...

from The Maximus Poems *(University of California Press, 1983)*

12. Arthur Rimbaud

Insouciant me, fermenting large waves,
yep, cried a lot; there was one cloud
looked like people from Colombia.
Saw snakes, icebergs, dancing phosphorus, blue floats.
I'm one big happy water sculpture
I'm a buttered flower stuck on the floor
I'm a glacier of hysterics
rubbing my sore shiny feet
which I call the two Maries.
Yep, naked
& stronger than alcohol
the wind gets old
gets picky about trees
sits down on the riverbank
& curses the tropics.
All aboard Leviathan!
The fare is a million golden birds
or tears shed in Europe.

From my translation of various lines from "Le bateau ivre"

13. Leonel Rugama

Expelled from the
promised land, in English,
not old, smooth
like the woods of Borneo
which would have cost a lot of money.

Here, an error is paid
for in blood, or who
knows what?

Son of this
son of that, son
of a bitch.

I'm going home
where there are tortillas.
I'll open my mouth &
put my hand in the fire.
That hand found a stone
& made seven poems of it &
a friend said they weren't bad
compared to the stone.

Nobody said nothing
to a grenade.
Six more than nothing
Julio was born here
lived with the saints
brought light
to a shack.

from La Tierra Es un Satélite de la Luna *(Editorial Nueva Nicaragua, 1983)*

14. Archbishop Oscar Romero

Let no one
document
a desert strewn with god.
Absorb
the projects of history.
It's all right.
It's alright.
It is alright.
Illuminate our tragic
peasants.
Looting
was assassinated.
The campus
the dawn
the day
itself
caught inside
on tv.
The rubbish dump
issued a press release.
The spokesman
the thumbs
their homes
exhumed
their bodies ·
tied behind their backs.
I would like to make a special appeal
an abomination
I implore
I beg
I order:

stop
liberation!
We have studied
today,
its hope,
its strength.

from the last homily delivered by Oscar Romero, in March 1980

15. Salvador Allende

Surely antennas
do not have bitterness
they have force—
people make history
deposited in a man,
the mother who knew.
History will judge
the calm metal instrument
of my voice.
I will always be next to
loyal, defend, riddled,
go forward
long live
these are
my last words!

from the last radio broadcast by Salvador Allende, in September 1973

My Knee Transplant

a cento

Ugh, what poisonous fumes & clouds
in short supply this year,
we're good & damaged.
I hear the bathtub filling
like a lightning silver suppository I clip through
for your unsatisfied enthusiasm.

My neighbour marches in his room,
he died, but luckily not in hospital, of a sunset or a drug,
of Orangina bottles,
of his only friend, dinner plate in his lips,
isn't that it? Honey, not us? Even now?
Or is it me?

Après le déluge

After the flood a horizontal president tugged his red coverlet.
After the flood seven translucent guppies of the right ate a striped cat.
After the flood one black bird on a black highway spoke French.
After the flood my car wore a brown moose for a hat.
After the flood two slices of smoked salmon crawled off with my lap.
After the flood my eyes fled like purple nebulae.

Hey Genet

after Stuart Ross after George Trakl

Yowza! Interstellar anaesthesia cures nova!
He stands at the end of this flat earth, looking both ways &
The score is in overtime.
Its average weight, however, could be a moon less, or more
Lurking by the dock at midnite, craves one last drunken sailor
Until they waken, & tumesce.
Wider, widest & disappears
With victim envy.

We are, after all
A bunch of bananas arguing about opposable hoofs!

At Lunch with Phyllis Gottlieb as She Thought of Writing *Sunburst*

Hot air pouring devils,
its huge, thick hose
reaches into the suck smoke is.
Gas masks what I know.
The café sat there
contemplating a young girl
—she's reading us— Phyllis whispers,
her serious hand
she's dark, darkle, darkishness
little fingers bade radioluminescence worship her,
but she is gone, gone, gone.
I gotta go, we both say at once.

Warning Sign Inside the Orbit of Mars

A monkey flew into space, a dog flew after him, a bunch of men flew after them, we made 17 footsteps on the moon & retreated, there's a bunch of guys & a few women in a fishing hut at the top edge of air, behold these works & tremble, giant gas-bags of Saturn!

4 a.m., Barcelona, Las Ramblas

after Charles Simic

A smell offers me its sister,
my severed finger hides under a wheel,
licking a cleaver coated in fur,
embedded in my palm.

A feral hamster dancing in a child's room,
in the west, a vision of the east,
using only his tongue,
as they starve.

Not touching this body,
the only method of entry,
by Thursday,
by holy Thursday.

After "Gasta Claus," by Ska-P

The revolution never came north,
they went south instead,
went further south,
then fell off the planet,
with all of us intact,
but little to breathe, less to eat, and there we float, just off to the left,
off the planet
watching the earth
like a tv you want to punch
cause the show sucks
and there's nothing else allowed on,
no stars that you want to follow,
and how do we get back,
how,
by words or deeds,
or just by wishing,
the hands out trying,
we are trying to pull ourselves back to the earth,
by grasping at the lack of molecules
into which we fell,
and if we get there,
we'll crawl up from the south,
like monsters,
we'll come north from the south
like monsters,
and norther
from souther,
and maybe you'll see us—

we look a little hungry,
not much to eat
in space.

Happy Birthday, Nicanor Parra!

The past eliminates all witnesses.

A real poet would break this line somewhere else.

You have not filled out this poem correctly.

Notes and Acknowledgements

My Own History of the War: The Ebro is the largest river in Spain. Site of many battles during the Spanish Civil War.

We Are Berias: Beria was the most influential of Stalin's secret police chiefs.

97 Lines: One line for each year of Nicanor's life (up to now).

& Ten Lines for Sara Gonzalez: Sara, who founded the Cuban *nueva trova* song movement along with Silvio Rodríguez and Pablo Milanés, died in Havana on February 2, 2012 at 62 years old. In 1987 she declared that my friendship with her group was *"pernicioso."*

Experiment to Demonstrate the Pact of Forgetting: The "pact of forgetting" is the unspoken "agreement" attributed to the Spanish people to not look too deeply into the past, primarily the Spanish Civil War, secondarily Franco's horrific 36-year dictatorship. Honoured by the left, enforced by the right, its newest victim is Judge Garzón, recently banned from being a judge for having opened an inquiry into mass murders during the Spanish Civil War.

At the Lenox Montparnasse Room 37: The Lenox, our favourite hotel in Paris, was the first residence of Man Ray when he arrived in that city.

Parliamentary Suite: In a move worthy of a Stalin or a Franco, Prime Minister Harper shut down Parliament for two months at the end of 2009 to avoid questions and an inquiry.

John Milton: Michael Fleishman was a beloved friend and fellow toiler in the fields of the law. He died suddenly at 62 during my trip to Chile in 2010.

Christ, Elqui: I continue my lifelong project of anti-translating Nicanor Parra's work. Parra's *Sermones y Prédicas del Cristo de Elqui* is a long poem published in 1977. Cristo de Elqui (Domingo Zárate Vega) was a Chilean peasant who wandered Chile's Elqui Valley starting around 1931, claiming, among other things, to be Christ returned, and to have had divine visitations. This anti-translation bears only a distant relation. These are selections from a larger work. Remember, as Parra said to me in Las Cruces in February, 2012, translation is treason.

Exit Interviews: These works are all dictation. Every word is found somewhere in the work cited.

*　*　*

Earlier versions of some of these poems appeared in *This Magazine, The Puritan* and *Rogue Stimulus: The Stephen Harper Holiday Anthology for a Prorogued Parliament* (Mansfield Press, 2010). I thank the editors and publishers of each for their good taste.

A version of "Exit Interviews" appeared as a limited edition, hand-sewn chapbook from Ottawa's inspired Apt. 9 Press in June, 2011. Go, Cameron!

Thanks and a hug to the great Chilean painter Eugenio Tellez for the use of his painting *El Asalto de la Máquina a las Fuerzas de la Destrucción* (2006) as my cover image. Check out his website, eugeniotellez.com, for more of his work.

Without the friendship and faith of Stuart Ross, this book would not have existed. Without the dogged determination and unlikely good humour of publisher Denis De Klerck, it would not be in your hands right now. Bless them both.

And bless Bella.

Of course, all my work is really dedicated to Jo-Anne.

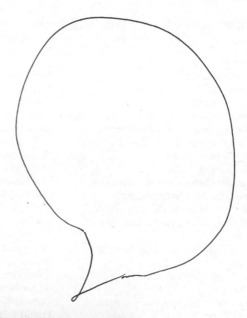

Jim Smith's last collection from Mansfield Press, 2009's *Back Off, Assassin! New and Selected Poems*, was longlisted for the 2010 Governor General's Award for Poetry, and hit # 7 on the Chapters/Indigo 14 Best Poetry Books for National Poetry Month 2010. During Jim's visit with antipoet Nicanor Parra in Las Cruces, Chile, in February 2012, Nicanor advised him that translation is "treason." In 61 years, Smith has published some 15 books and chapbooks of poetry, ran a small literary magazine and press, went to law school late and litigates for a living in Toronto.

Other Books from Mansfield Press

Poetry

Leanne Averbach, *Fever*
Nelson Ball, *In This Thin Rain*
Stephen Brockwell & Stuart Ross, eds.,
Rogue Stimulus: The Stephen Harper Holiday Anthology for a Prorogued Parliament
Diana Fitzgerald Bryden, *Learning Russian*
Alice Burdick, *Flutter*
Alice Burdick, *Holler*
Margaret Christakos, *wipe.under.a.love*
Pino Coluccio, *First Comes Love*
Gary Michael Dault, *The Milk of Birds*
Pier Giorgio Di Cicco, *The Dark Time of Angels*
Pier Giorgio Di Cicco, *Dead Men of the Fifties*
Pier Giorgio Di Cicco, *The Honeymoon Wilderness*
Pier Giorgio Di Cicco, *Living in Paradise*
Pier Giorgio Di Cicco, *Early Works*
Pier Giorgio Di Cicco, *The Visible World*
Salvatore Difalco, *What Happens at Canals*
Christopher Doda, *Aesthetics Lesson*
Christopher Doda, *Among Ruins*
Rishma Dunlop, *The Body of My Garden*
Rishma Dunlop, *Lover Through Departure: New and Selected Poems*
Rishma Dunlop, *Metropolis*
Rishma Dunlop & Priscila Uppal, eds., *Red Silk: An Anthology of South Asian Women Poets*
Ollivier Dyens, *The Profane Earth*
Jaime Forsythe, *Sympathy Loophole*
Carole Glasser Langille, *Late in a Slow Time*
Suzanne Hancock, *Another Name for Bridge*
Jason Heroux, *Emergency Hallelujah*
Jason Heroux, *Memoirs of an Alias*
Jason Heroux, *Natural Capital*
John B. Lee, *In the Terrible Weather of Guns*
Jeanette Lynes, *The Aging Cheerleader's Alphabet*
David W. McFadden, *Be Calm, Honey*
David W. McFadden, *What's the Score?*
Leigh Nash, *Goodbye, Ukulele*
Lillian Necakov, *The Bone Broker*
Lillian Necakov, *Hooligans*

Peter Norman, *At the Gates of the Theme Park*
Natasha Nuhanovic, *Stray Dog Embassy*
Catherine Owen & Joe Rosenblatt, with Karen Moe, *Dog*
Corrado Paina, *The Alphabet of the Traveler*
Corrado Paina, *The Dowry of Education*
Corrado Paina, *Hoarse Legend*
Corrado Paina, *Souls in Plain Clothes*
Matt Santateresa, *A Beggar's Loom*
Matt Santateresa, *Icarus Redux*
Ann Shin, *The Last Thing Standing*
Jim Smith, *Back Off, Assassin! New and Selected Poems*
Robert Earl Stewart, *Campfire Radio Rhapsody*
Robert Earl Stewart, *Something Burned on the Southern Border*
Carey Toane, *The Crystal Palace*
Priscila Uppal, *Winter Sport: Poems*
Steve Venright, *Floors of Enduring Beauty*
Brian Wickers, *Stations of the Lost*

Fiction

Marianne Apostolides, *The Lucky Child*
Sarah Dearing, *The Art of Sufficient Conclusions*
Denis De Klerck, ed., *Particle & Wave: A Mansfield Omnibus of Electro-Magnetic Fiction*
Paula Eisenstein, *Flip Turn*
Marko Sijan, *Mongrel*
Tom Walmsley, *Dog Eat Rat*

Non-Fiction

George Bowering, *How I Wrote Certain of My Books*
Denis De Klerck & Corrado Paina, eds., *College Street–Little Italy: Toronto's Renaissance Strip*
Pier Giorgio Di Cicco, *Municipal Mind: Manifestos for the Creative City*
Amy Lavender Harris, *Imagining Toronto*

To order Mansfield Press titles online, please visit mansfieldpress.net